In Celebration of

_____

_____

Date

_____

Guest Name
(address/phone #/email)

Notes

_____

_____

_____

_____

_____

_____

_____

_____

_____

_____

_____

_____

_____

Guest Name
(address/phone #/email)

Notes

_____

_____

_____

_____

_____

_____

_____

_____

_____

_____

_____

_____

_____

_____

Guest Name
(address/phone #/email)

Notes

Guest Name
(address/phone #/email)

Notes

_____

_____

_____

_____

_____

_____

_____

_____

_____

_____

_____

_____

_____

_____

_____

_____

Guest Name
(address/phone #/email)

Notes

_____

_____

_____

_____

Guest Name
(address/phone #/email)

Notes

_____

_____

_____

_____

_____

_____

_____

_____

_____

_____

_____

_____

_____

_____

_____

Guest Name
(address/phone #/email)

Notes

Guest Name
(address/phone #/email)

Notes

_____

_____

_____

_____

_____

_____

_____

_____

_____

_____

_____

_____

_____

_____

Guest Name
(address/phone #/email)

Notes

_____

_____

_____

_____

_____

_____

_____

_____

_____

_____

_____

_____

_____

_____

Guest Name
(address/phone #/email)

Notes

Guest Name
(address/phone #/email)

Notes

Guest Name
(address/phone #/email)

Notes

Guest Name
(address/phone #/email)

Notes

_____

_____

_____

_____

_____

_____

_____

_____

_____

_____

_____

_____

_____

_____

_____

Guest Name
(address/phone #/email)

Notes

Guest Name
(address/phone #/email)

Notes

_____

_____

_____

_____

Guest Name
(address/phone #/email)

Notes

Guest Name
(address/phone #/email)

Notes

Guest Name
(address/phone #/email)

Notes

Guest Name
(address/phone #/email)

Notes

_____

_____

_____

_____

_____

_____

_____

_____

_____

_____

_____

_____

_____

Guest Name
(address/phone #/email)

Notes

Guest Name
(address/phone #/email)

Notes

_____

_____

_____

_____

Guest Name
(address/phone #/email)

Notes

_____

_____

_____

_____

_____

_____

_____

_____

_____

_____

_____

_____

_____

_____

_____

Guest Name
(address/phone #/email)

Notes

Guest Name
(address/phone #/email)

Notes

_____

_____

_____

_____

_____

_____

_____

_____

_____

_____

_____

_____

_____

_____

Guest Name
(address/phone #/email)

Notes

_____

_____

_____

_____

_____

_____

_____

_____

_____

_____

_____

_____

Guest Name
(address/phone #/email)

Notes

_____

_____

_____

_____

_____

_____

_____

_____

_____

_____

_____

_____

_____

_____

Guest Name
(address/phone #/email)

Notes

_____

_____

_____

_____

Guest Name
(address/phone #/email)

Notes

Guest Name
(address/phone #/email)

Notes

_____

_____

_____

_____

_____

_____

_____

_____

_____

_____

_____

_____

_____

_____

_____

Guest Name
(address/phone #/email)

Notes

Guest Name
(address/phone #/email)

Notes

_____

_____

_____

_____

Guest Name
(address/phone #/email)

Notes

Guest Name
(address/phone #/email)

Notes

_____

_____

_____

_____

_____

_____

_____

_____

_____

_____

_____

_____

_____

_____

Guest Name
(address/phone #/email)

Notes

Guest Name
(address/phone #/email)

Notes

Guest Name
(address/phone #/email)

Notes

Guest Name
(address/phone #/email)

Notes

Guest Name
(address/phone #/email)

Notes

Guest Name
(address/phone #/email)

Notes

_____

_____

_____

_____

_____

_____

_____

_____

_____

_____

_____

_____

Guest Name
(address/phone #/email)

Notes

Guest Name
(address/phone #/email)

Notes

Guest Name
(address/phone #/email)

Notes

_____

_____

_____

_____

_____

_____

_____

_____

_____

_____

_____

_____

_____

Guest Name
(address/phone #/email)

Notes

Guest Name
(address/phone #/email)

Notes

_____

_____

_____

_____

_____

_____

_____

_____

_____

_____

_____

_____

_____

_____

Guest Name
(address/phone #/email)

Notes

Guest Name
(address/phone #/email)

Notes

Guest Name
(address/phone #/email)

Notes

Guest Name
(address/phone #/email)

Notes

Guest Name
(address/phone #/email)

Notes

_____

_____

_____

_____

_____

_____

_____

_____

_____

_____

_____

_____

_____

_____

Guest Name
(address/phone #/email)

Notes

_____

_____

_____

_____

Guest Name

(address/phone #/email)

Notes

_____

_____

_____

_____

_____

_____

_____

_____

_____

_____

_____

_____

_____

Guest Name
(address/phone #/email)

Notes

Guest Name
(address/phone #/email)

Notes

Guest Name
(address/phone #/email)

Notes

Guest Name
(address/phone #/email)

Notes

_____

_____

_____

_____

_____

_____

_____

_____

_____

_____

_____

_____

_____

Guest Name
(address/phone #/email)

Notes

_____

_____

_____

_____

_____

_____

_____

_____

_____

_____

_____

_____

_____

Guest Name
(address/phone #/email)

Notes

Guest Name
(address/phone #/email)

Notes

Guest Name
(address/phone #/email)

Notes

_____

_____

_____

_____

_____

_____

_____

_____

_____

_____

_____

_____

_____

Guest Name
(address/phone #/email)

Notes

Guest Name
(address/phone #/email)

Notes

_____

_____

_____

_____

_____

_____

_____

_____

_____

_____

_____

_____

_____

_____

Guest Name
(address/phone #/email)

Notes

_____

_____

_____

_____

_____

_____

_____

_____

_____

_____

_____

_____

_____

_____

Guest Name
(address/phone #/email)

Notes

_____

_____

_____

_____

_____

_____

_____

_____

_____

_____

_____

_____

_____

Guest Name
(address/phone #/email)

Notes

Guest Name
(address/phone #/email)

Notes

(address/phone #/email)

Guest Name
(address/phone #/email)

Notes

_____

_____

_____

_____

Guest Name
(address/phone #/email)

Notes

Guest Name
(address/phone #/email)

Notes

_____

_____

_____

_____

_____

_____

_____

_____

_____

_____

_____

_____

_____

Guest Name
(address/phone #/email)

Notes

Guest Name
(address/phone #/email)

Notes

Guest Name
(address/phone #/email)

Notes

Guest Name
(address/phone #/email)

Notes

Guest Name
(address/phone #/email)

Notes

Guest Name
(address/phone #/email)

Notes

Guest Name
(address/phone #/email)

Notes

Guest Name
(address/phone #/email)

Notes

Guest Name
(address/phone #/email)

Notes

Guest Name
(address/phone #/email)

Notes

_____

_____

_____

_____

_____

_____

_____

_____

_____

_____

_____

_____

_____

_____

Guest Name
(address/phone #/email)

Notes

Guest Name
(address/phone #/email)

Notes

Guest Name
(address/phone #/email)

Notes

Guest Name
(address/phone #/email)

Notes

_____

_____

_____

_____

_____

_____

_____

_____

_____

_____

_____

_____

_____

_____

_____

Guest Name
(address/phone #/email)

Notes

Guest Name

(address/phone #/email)

Notes

Guest Name
(address/phone #/email)

Notes

Guest Name
(address/phone #/email)

Notes

_____

_____

_____

_____

Guest Name
(address/phone #/email)

Notes

_____

_____

_____

_____

Guest Name
(address/phone #/email)

Notes

Guest Name
(address/phone #/email)

Notes

Guest Name
(address/phone #/email)

Notes

_____

_____

_____

_____

_____

_____

_____

_____

_____

_____

_____

_____

_____

_____

Guest Name
(address/phone #/email)

Notes

Guest Name
(address/phone #/email)

Notes

_____

_____

_____

_____

_____

_____

_____

_____

_____

_____

_____

_____

_____

_____

Guest Name
(address/phone #/email)

Notes

Guest Name
(address/phone #/email)

Notes

Guest Name
(address/phone #/email)

Notes

_____

_____

_____

_____

Guest Name
(address/phone #/email)

Notes

_____

_____

_____

_____

_____

_____

_____

_____

_____

_____

_____

Guest Name
(address/phone #/email)

Notes

_____

_____

_____

_____

_____

_____

_____

_____

_____

_____

_____

_____

_____

Guest Name
(address/phone #/email)

Notes

Guest Name
(address/phone #/email)

Notes

Guest Name
(address/phone #/email)

Notes

Guest Name
(address/phone #/email)

Notes

_____

_____

_____

_____

Guest Name
(address/phone #/email)

Notes

_____

_____

_____

_____

_____

_____

_____

_____

_____

_____

_____

_____

_____

Guest Name
(address/phone #/email)

Notes

_____

_____

_____

_____

_____

_____

_____

_____

_____

_____

_____

_____

_____

Guest Name
(address/phone #/email)

Notes

Guest Name
(address/phone #/email)

Notes

Guest Name
(address/phone #/email)

Notes

Guest Name
(address/phone #/email)

Notes

Guest Name
(address/phone #/email)

Notes

Guest Name
(address/phone #/email)

Notes

Guest Name
(address/phone #/email)

Notes

Made in the USA
Middletown, DE
24 September 2023

39223870R00066